The
Promise

Joy Through t ‸‸‸‸ *ness*

Sandy Schronce
with Bruce & Ethan Schronce

The Promise

Copyright © 2020 by Sandy Schronce

Dedications & Acknowledgments

To my husband Bruce, who is my best friend and soul mate. You are one of the godliest men I know, and I thank God for bringing us together so many years ago.

I love you beyond words.

To my two sons, Ethan and Hunter. Through our ups and downs, you both have helped shape me into the woman God purposed me to be. I love you with all my heart and couldn't be a prouder Mama Bear!

To Victoria – "My Daughter" – As I have told you on many occasions, you are definitely an answered prayer. I thank God for bringing you into Ethan's life at just the right time and for becoming his wife and a daughter to Bruce and me. We love you.

To Jesse – Thank you for loving our son Hunter unconditionally. You taught him and me what "unconditional love" looks like. For that I will be eternally grateful. No matter what the future holds, Bruce and I will always think of you like a daughter. Keep trusting God's plans for your life.

To my friends and family – There are too many to name, but you know who you are. Thank you for all your love and support through some very hard and difficult years. Your words of encouragement, phone calls, cards and especially your prayers are what helped get us through the dark valleys and experience true joy on the other side. I love you and thank God for you.

I would like to thank everyone who had a part in bringing our story to life, whether it involved transcribing written words to the computer (Kathy V. Cruz), content editing (Mary A. Felkins, author of inspirational romance and devotions at www.maryfelkins.com), or praying us through it. Your time and devotion have been such a blessing and there are no words to describe my gratitude.

Contents

Introduction

◦ *Sandy* ◦

I am excited and overwhelmed to share my story with you. When God confirmed He wanted me to write my story, I felt like Moses when God asked him to go to Pharaoh and bring the Israelites out of Egypt. Moses' response was, "Who am I...?" Like me, he considered himself very inadequate for the task.

Even though Moses had his doubts, he chose to be obedient to God's assignment. I, too, have chosen to step out in faith and trust that God will take my messy, jumbled up words and create a beautiful story that reflects His love.

The following chapters include unique perspectives from me, Bruce, and our son Ethan though the story is the same.

I hope you will be able to see how God has made "our"

story come together as "one" in Him. My prayer is for you to experience God's love, peace and joy as you walk with my family and me through our "Journey of Brokenness."

God Speaks

◊ Bruce ◊

*"Then you will call on me and come and pray to me,
and I will listen to you. You will seek me and find me
when you seek me with all your heart..."*

Jeremiah 29:12-14 (NIV)

Several years ago, I was sitting at my kitchen table praying to God in frustration. I don't even remember what brought me to this point, but I mentally shouted, "God, if you really want to talk to me, why don't you make it easier for me to hear you?" In that moment, I felt God whisper into my soul, "Because I love you, and I don't want you to settle for less than what I have for you. I want to teach you My ways, and My ways are greater than yours."

The Promise

"For my thoughts are not your thoughts, neither are your ways my ways," declares the Lord.

Isaiah 55:8 (NIV)

Looking back, I realized God had been teaching me through the years how to listen and trust Him in all circumstances. But I also came to understand that He was not just answering my questions, giving me guidance or teaching me how to get through difficult times. He was showing me His true nature and how much He loved me. His ultimate desire was that I would experience this love to the fullest. However, if I only speak to God on my terms, wanting to hear from my perspective based on my agenda, I will miss the true experience of the relationships for which we are all created. I will be more focused on the blessings of God and miss the greatest gift of all - His presence!

Knowing God loves and speaks to me reassures me of His presence. I am comforted by His peace and how He leads me in His power. It's important that you understand this as I share some markers in my life where God has spoken in very real and intimate ways which have shaped the story we now share.

Sandy and I have liked each other since the second grade and dated all through high school and most of college. I always felt God had given Sandy to me and that she would one day be my wife. But when we were in college, we broke up, and it looked like she would move in a direction that didn't include me. I was crushed! This would be the first great pain of my life. I can remember driving away from her house, pulling to the side of the road and banging on the steering wheel in absolute brokenness. (I'm amazed how strong steering wheels are.) Being at the end of myself, I did the only thing I knew to do. I prayed and gave it over to God. I told God I didn't understand what was happening, but I trusted Him, regardless of the outcome. God assured me that His ways are best, and His promises are fulfilled as long as I am willing to surrender to His will rather than force mine. Long story short, we're on our thirty-fifth year of marriage, and she still rocks my world! This was one of my first real tests of seeking God and trusting His plans for my life.

Another area of my life I entrusted to God was my vocational calling. Early in my business career I was a successful executive in the furniture industry. The money was great. I was recognized for my leadership, and the opportunities seemed endless. I believed I was right where I was supposed to be. Then things began to change. I sensed God was awakening me to something deep —and dormant—in my soul which awaited God's timing. God was telling me, "There's more you need to know about Me and My purposes for you, and it's time to move. Will you trust Me"? This was confusing, and I didn't understand where God was leading, but after two years of praying (often begging God to leave me where I was), I surrendered and agreed to go wherever He led.

The next thing I knew I was trading the business world for a life of ministry. That was nowhere on my radar! Why would God move me from something I enjoyed and was good at to place me where I had no vocational experience? I didn't want to go. Why ministry? At the time I wasn't sure why or how it would happen, but He made a way and I served seven years as Executive Pastor where I attended church for seventeen years.

I later came to realize this calling was a critical time of equipping me for what would come next. As a pastor, I received a bachelor's in religious education, a master's in leadership and became certified as a Life and Leadership Coach. It turned out, ministry wasn't the end either but just another piece of the puzzle. God then led me to create the for-profit business of StrongLead, LLC and the not-for-profit organization of Catawba Valley Leadership Foundation. Each would serve to develop, support and connect strong leaders founded on principles God was teaching me through experiences of both business and ministry.

I won't detail the entire journey, but I could have never gotten to the place I am today without trusting God. The vision He gave me would become my true calling.

The bottom line is: God loves me. He speaks to me. I can trust Him no matter what.

But would I?

A Family Bond

◦ *Bruce* ◦

Aside from my salvation and relationship with God, nothing is more precious to me than my family. I have my beautiful wife, Sandy, our two amazing sons, Ethan and Hunter, an incredible daughter-in-law, Victoria, whom we claim as our own daughter, and even great extended families on both sides. For our immediate family, some of our most enjoyable things in life have been worshipping together, camping trips, watching Friday night movies and eating pizza, coaching and watching the boys in sports, taking father-son business trips to the big cities, big family get-togethers and just simply loving, laughing and hanging out together.

But families can also be a source of great heartache. Years ago, I had done a study on the word "fellowship" and discovered the root word terminology actually meant "suffering together." Considering the closeness of our family, we were taken on an unforeseen path we never saw coming. This journey shattered the comfortable and familiar world we knew and brought us to a plentiful place of "suffering together."

It is often said, "Boys will be boys." But due to their adventurous spirits, both of ours tasted the fruits of a dark world that took us for an unexpected ride. That ride started with Ethan in high school and escalated when he went to college. There was partying, drinking, marijuana... a life out of control. It was directionless. Obviously, Sandy and I were crushed. We tried everything we knew to help him see that the path he was on would end up in a place he didn't want to go. Nothing we said seemed to matter.

Sandy and I were at our wits end and felt helpless. As I prayed, God spoke very clearly, asking me to trust Him with Ethan's life. He taught me to let go and led me through various conversations with Ethan through which God Himself began to work in Ethan's life. Transformation began to take place.

During Ethan's sophomore year of college, he was broken after he turned in his last paper of the semester. As it was pouring down rain, he got into his car and heard God clearly ask him, *"Where are you Ethan?"* Ethan began crying uncontrollably, called me for help, and repented to God. The next semester he transferred to a different college and began a new life in Christ that has led him to experience blessings beyond his imagination.

Hunter's story unfolds a little differently. Like Ethan, Hunter loved life and life loved him right back. However, his experiences took him down a dangerously different road that introduced him to opioids. His choices led him into a life of addiction with horrifying consequences. Our family was turned upside down by circumstances that came so fast and furious that we barely knew which end was up. We had never experienced anything so devasting and out of control. We found ourselves in a seemingly hopeless and helpless place wondering how we got here and where and when it would end.

The battle had only begun, and it was greater than our faith had ever experienced. It was a battle for the heart and soul that included heartache, desperation, tears, yelling, pleading, discipline, rehab, counseling, prayer, and the hardest conversations and decisions Sandy and I would ever face. Our conversations included, "What if this darkness takes his life?" and decisions that would force our beloved son out of our home. But above all else, we turned to God, and we were unified in our faith.

On Father's Day of 2017, Hunter gave me a CD of a song he had written and recorded called "Da Rad Dad." I was absolutely blown away because it sounded so good and because of the way he honored and thanked me for being a godly dad. But beyond those reasons, his lyrics acknowledged and pointed others to our heavenly Father. I couldn't have felt more loved, honored, blessed and proud, especially in light of where Hunter had been. The song would later affirm —once again— how much God loved me and my family and how He was giving us great gifts to remind us of this, even before they would be needed the most.

Da Rad Dad song

Letting Go

◦ *Sandy* ◦

I don't know about you, but for me, the two words "Letting go" have been extremely hard to do in my life... especially when it involved my boys, Ethan and Hunter. Bruce and I love them with all our heart, but truth be told, there have been many times throughout the years we wanted to strangle them (out of love, of course!). Both our boys accepted Christ and were baptized at an early age. As a family we worshipped together, prayed together and ministered together. We were a close-knit family, and all seemed wonderful... until the teenage/high school years. Both Ethan and Hunter went through some dark, rebellious times.

The word "control" (defined as the power to influence or direct people's behavior or the course of events) was high on my parenting list for all the right reasons. I wanted to protect my boys from harm and keep them from making bad decisions that could affect their future and the plans God had for them. "For I know the plans I have for you," declares the LORD, "plans to prosper you and not to harm you, plans to give you hope and a future." Jeremiah 29:11 (NIV). However, the more I tried to control, the further they drifted away. Our oldest son Ethan turned back toward God during his sophomore year in college. He is married to a precious young lady, Victoria, whom we love and adore. Bruce and I have a wonderful relationship with both of them. We are so blessed to watch the two of them pursuing God together.

Hunter's story, however, reads a bit differently. I would like to share a few up close and personal struggles that our family has had to endure because of one very ugly word... addiction!

Addiction is a sickness that not only affects the addict but everyone who is a part of their life (especially family). Throughout Hunter's story, God taught me to stop trying to control and to truly "Let go" and trust Him regardless of the circumstances.

As previously mentioned, Hunter had accepted Christ at a young age and loved sharing about Jesus. On a mission trip he'd be the first one to knock on a door and invite the kids to Vacation Bible School. I recall one mission trip to Tennessee when Hunter was about ten years old. He and another friend helped lead a boy to accept Christ. They explained what it meant to become a Christian and prayed with him. It made my Mama heart smile to see how God was using him at such an early age. Hunter would lay in bed at night as we said our prayers, and he would cry for his friends. He wanted all his friends to know Jesus.

He had a saying he often repeated ... "I Love My Life!." And he truly meant it. His personality and smile lit up a room. He was fun-loving and carefree. He never met a stranger. He truly loved everyone, and everyone loved him.

During Hunter's sophomore year in high school, Bruce and I began to notice some changes in his behavior. This is where the story became dark and continued so for many years. Hunter began to experiment with underage drinking and smoking marijuana. What started out as a "fun time" with his friends took him and our family down a very dark road. Two months shy of his twentieth birthday, Hunter acknowledged he had a problem with pain killers (opioids) and needed help. Through a friend of mine we were able to find a Christian men's rehab facility in Southern Georgia from where her own son had graduated. Hunter did everything he was required to do to get accepted into the program. Two weeks later, we drove five hours from our hometown in North Carolina to the facility where we dropped him off for a twelve month stay. The staff informed us Hunter was not permitted to leave and we could not have any contact with him for the first three months. After that, we could write letters and visit on weekends with permission. So, over the next year, Bruce, Ethan and I made the long road trip every three weeks to see him. The property was an old, smelly, moldy schoolhouse, but our family made the most of it and just enjoyed being together.

On Sundays we were able to attend church with him which was awesome. We did a lot of laughing and crying over those short, sweet visits. Healing was taking place in all of us. It broke my heart every time we had to say good-bye, but I knew it was best. Hunter was getting the help and tools he needed to overcome his struggles. He rededicated his life to the Lord while there and began seeking God's plan and purpose for his life. He wanted to share his testimony and help others (especially teens) to see the truth behind the drugs.

A month shy of his twenty-first birthday, he finished the program. Our family was very proud and excited to see what the future would hold for Hunter. I was so thankful that all the "bad stuff" and heartache was behind us and thought we could finally move on with life... be normal again! Oh, how sadly mistaken I was. The next two years of my life were anything but normal.

After only one month, Hunter relapsed. Unfortunately this relapse wasn't a one-time deal. It was the beginning of some of the most painful, agonizing and hurtful heartaches I have ever had to experience.

Hunter knew how much his dad and I loved him, but he also knew we had boundaries and would not tolerate him doing drugs while living under our roof. Bruce and I sought God's guidance constantly, and we both had peace about how to handle each situation that arose. "...as for me and my household, we will serve the LORD." Joshua 24:15 (NIV). We knew we could not and should not be an enabler to Hunter's addiction. He knew if he chose to do drugs there would be consequences.

Several times we had to make the extremely difficult decision to have Hunter pack his bags and leave our home. As a parent, it is heart-wrenching to watch your grown child walk out of your house with only a backpack to his name and not know where he's going or what will happen to him. On one such occasion, I was on my knees in my bedroom closet, face down to the ground, tears rolling down my cheeks, grasping for air, crying out to God to watch over my son. I was so distraught and felt so hopeless. I had no idea what else to do to help Hunter and had reached the end of my rope... I was broken. I was *truly* broken!

As I continued to cry out for help that evening, God met me exactly where I was... in my closet, on my knees, face down, in a state of hopelessness. In that moment, God's Spirit began to speak to me about changing the way I prayed for Hunter. Instead of praying for what I wanted to see happen or what I thought needed to happen, God was asking me to "Let go" of

15

my plans, to pray specifically: "God's will be done" and to trust the plans He had for Hunter and our family.

Over the next several months I disciplined myself to pray, "God's will be done, not mine!" Once I grasped the power and significance of those words, I experienced a precious freedom like never before. I was finally able to "Let go" and trust God's plans... regardless.

Needless to say, Ethan was impacted by all this as well. He loved his little brother and wanted the best for him. Hunter admired Ethan and looked up to him as a role model. When Hunter was in a good place, I loved watching the two of them together. They were constantly cracking jokes and making everyone laugh around them. It was genuine brotherly love!

When Ethan and Victoria became engaged, he asked Hunter to be his best man. Hunter was so excited. Two weeks before the wedding, the four of us planned to take a family vacation in Florida. Hunter had been clean for several months and seemed to be doing well. The night before we were leaving, Bruce and I were in bed and heard Hunter moving around in his room. We got up to see what was going on. He told us he needed to go meet someone. We could tell he had taken something because his speech was slurred, and he wasn't making sense. We tried to talk him into staying, but he was determined to go. We told him if he walked out the door, we were going to Florida without him and he would not be in his brother's wedding. But at that point, our words were ineffective. The addiction had taken over. He ran out the door and jumped in a car that was waiting for him in front of our house.

We were devastated but continued with our plans to fly to Florida the next morning without Hunter. The three of us enjoyed our time together, but we all felt a deep hurt and void.

As a result of Hunter's choice, Ethan made the very hard decision that Hunter would not be in his wedding. As a mom, I was crushed but, as always, God picked me up and put the pieces of my fragmented heart back together again.

With Ethan and Victoria's permission, Hunter came to the wedding but was not part of the wedding party. He felt great remorse and shame for what he had done and the pain he had caused his family. I remained hopeful the loss of being in his brother's wedding would be a wakeup call and he would see how much the drugs had stolen from him. But unfortunately, that was not the case.

Two months later on a Saturday morning, a friend of Hunter's showed up on our front porch. He said Hunter was in his car and was really bad off. He wasn't sure what he had taken, but he was unresponsive. Bruce and I rushed to the car to see our son turning blue. Bruce grabbed Hunter out of the car, and he just fell limp in his dad's arms. He was not breathing! Bruce yelled for me to call "911" while he frantically (but prayerfully) shook Hunter in hopes he'd start breathing again. After what seemed like an eternity, Hunter took a breath and slowly opened his eyes. When the ambulance arrived, they took him into the cab and administered Naloxone, a medication to rapidly reverse opioid overdose. Then they rushed him to the hospital. The doctors told us if the EMT had not administered Naloxone, Hunter's body would have shut down and he would have died. Because his liver count was so high, it was critical that they get the numbers down within the next twenty-four hours or he'd need a liver transplant. Thank God, over the next few days, his numbers returned to normal.

This was a huge wake up call for Hunter. He knew God had given him a second chance. He was so thankful to God, his family, and his girlfriend, Jesse, for not giving up on him and loving him unconditionally.

One and a half months later, Hunter wrote the following poem and gave it to his family as a Christmas present...

A FAMILY'S BOND

A bond to words can be a bond to love
A family's bond is all of the above
Peers come through and peers drive by
Yet a family never fades even when you don't try

Joy Through the Brokenness

You cry for joy and cry for a hand
Your family reaches out without demand
Kids forsaken become adults in pain
As adults in pain have problems the same
No pain no gain, as the tears all rain
Family's umbrella results in no shame
Love breaks bondage of every chain
Yet still love wonders when the aching will stop
A loved one lies with sand on top

As he fights and fights through sinking sand
The family all prays til he's safe on land
They hurt and scream through the painful sight
But never give up til the angels take flight
Love wins wars and love heals sores

But this unending love so rare to find
As a family's love is one of a kind
It remains through thin, persevering through thick
This love of family has healed the sick
Life on your own is life with no cause
And my family's still here despite my flaws
God's grace saved as family has too
So lucky and blessed for family so true
Thanks to the power of love, my life has a new view

The months following Christmas, Hunter did very well in his effort to stay clean. But as the story continues, it will become clear that God's plans are not always our plans. And even though God is faithful in His promises, they may look totally different than what we imagined...

God's will be done!

OK?

◦ *Sandy* ◦

In the spring of 2013, I decided to hang two humming-bird feeders near our screened porch. I had never had a desire before, but for some reason I felt an urgency to do this now. I frequently changed the sugar water in them, but for almost two months I never saw any hummingbirds. One day as I was praying for Hunter during a very difficult time, I sought reassurance from God and pleaded, "Please just let me see one hummingbird on the feeder to let me know that Hunter is going to be OK."

Well, within a few minutes there was a beautiful ruby-throated hummingbird on the feeder. I can't begin to de-scribe the joy and excitement I felt at that moment. I cried out to God, thanking Him for His promise... Hunter was going to be OK!

Over the next couple of weeks, I had not just one but four hummingbirds, and they have returned every spring since - reminding me of God's promise. Isn't that how God works? He always gives us more than we ask or deserve.

Here are a few more hummingbird stories.

I was over at a friend's house one day for prayer. She knew about my hummingbird promise and shared about a friend of hers who had found a hummingbird trapped in her garage near the window beside an open door but still couldn't find its way out. We both laughed about it and proceeded with our prayer time together. When we finished, I went to my car and checked my phone. I received a text message from Bruce with a picture of him holding a hummingbird in his hand. I called him immediately for an explanation. He said he had walked out in the garage and saw a hummingbird trapped at one of the tall windows. It was going crazy hitting itself against the glass trying to get out. The tiny little bird could see his freedom on the other side of the glass but was struggling to get there on his own. Bruce got a ladder, slowly climbed up, and began to talk to the frightened bird. As he continued to talk, it eventually calmed down enough for him to take it in hand and carry it down the ladder. As Bruce left the garage, he gently stroked the bird's head and took a couple of pictures. Eventually, the scared little hummingbird gained its composure and flew off to face yet another day of life's ups and downs.

As Bruce told me the story, God revealed that this hummingbird was like Hunter who could see where he needed to go but struggled to get there. Just like Bruce holding the hummingbird in his hand, God assured me that He had Hunter in His hand and he was going to be OK!

One day I went to my patio to talk to God and pray for Hunter. The patio is located off the screened-in porch and opposite my hummingbird feeders. Soon after I began to pray, a hummingbird flew so close to my head I could almost touch it. It just hovered right next to me as we stared at each other for what seemed like forever. Then, in the blink of an eye, it was gone. The encounter brought such peace to my heart, a little gift from God to assure me that He hears my prayers.

Ethan and Victoria's wedding was held at a lovely farm venue located in the foothills of western North Carolina. The photographer did an amazing job capturing the stories and memories of that special day. She was completely unaware of my hummingbird connections or the promise related to them. But a few weeks later as we were looking at all the gorgeous wedding photos, one made my heart skip. It was a beautiful closeup of a hummingbird sitting on a feeder. The photographer had no idea how much that picture would mean to us, but God did.

Here is the poem Hunter wrote me as a gift for Mother's Day, 2017...

A HUMMINGBIRD'S PROMISE

Wings untamed, and wings that remained
The wings so constant as was its peace
Unlike any other including the geese
Speaking so clearly to the heart of a mom
Whom ticks and tocks like a worrisome bomb
For where was the strength in this spineless creation
Floating in awe with a son's correlation
Is nectar the symbol of milk to a boy
Or the playful nature to a son with a toy
Yet this bird is much more to one looking to God

Joy Through the Brokenness

With fish of anxiety outweighing her rod
But she seeks and she weeps for her chick as a hen
As a bird just humming sent for her as a win
Singing a tune of hope from despair
This miracle bird so miraculously rare
Joy through troubles and love through wars
This mom kept believing in the son she adores
The promise of God was a promise from birds
Protecting a son through the cringing of curbs
As he fights and he runs from the truth to the lies
These birds kept dancing for her heart and her eyes
When all else failed they replenished her soul
As the fruits of the spirit began to take toll
Waiting in wonder when her child would come round
Until the day of resurrection when her son was then found

On Father's Day, 2017, I surprised Bruce with a cabin rental in Roan Mountain, Tennessee for our family to spend the weekend together. This place is very special to all of us. Bruce had taken Ethan and Hunter there for their birthdays and other occasions to spend some father and son time together. We had spent many weekends as a family at this mountain retreat hiking, playing games, sitting around a campfire and spending family time with God. There are fifteen cabins to rent, but we had never stayed in this particular cabin before.

As we were carrying our luggage into the cabin, Hunter yelled, "Mom, come here!" When I approached the bedroom where Bruce and I would be sleeping, I saw Hunter lying on the bed which had a bedspread with hummingbirds printed all over it and pictures of hummingbirds hanging on the wall. Hunter just looked at me and smiled his big beautiful smile. We both knew that God keeps His promises!

Even then, God was giving me His promise and preparing me and my family for what we were about to go through. You see, three weeks later our precious son, Hunter, at the age of twenty-three, passed on from an overdose on July 15, 2017...

As I collapsed in the middle of the street in front of Hunter's apartment, all I could do was to cry out to God, "But you gave me your promise, God. You gave me your promise that Hunter was going to be OK... Well, this doesn't look OK to me!"

The next morning, as Bruce and I were trying to process everything, we were sitting in our screened porch watching the hummingbirds, and I began to read Hunter's hummingbird poem silently while Bruce was praying aloud. I questioned God again, "But you gave me your promise over and over that Hunter was going to be OK. And this doesn't look OK to me!" As I continued to question God, looking at the poem and listening to Bruce pray, God so clearly said, "Sandy, I gave you that promise four years ago for this very moment, so that you would know Hunter is OK because he is with Me now... He is more than OK!"

You see, my OK and God's OK looked totally different. I thought Hunter was going to be OK here on this earth, that God was going to heal him and use his testimony, particularly his music, to reach others since it was his heart and passion to help people overcome addiction. Hunter loved writing song lyrics and composing music. He probably wrote over one hundred songs, three of which he recorded before he passed. But needless to say, God knew Hunter wasn't going to be able to overcome his addiction completely so God's OK was to take Hunter home and use his —and our— story in a different way. God loved Hunter so much He took him out of this crazy world and gave him peace. God knew Hunter was going to struggle with this sickness for the rest of his life, so in His loving grace and mercy He freed Hunter and us, his family, from endless heartache and suffering on earth. We are FREE with Hunter!

Remember Hunter's saying growing up, "I love my life"? When the addiction took over, he didn't say that anymore. But I know now without a doubt he is saying, "I love my life" louder than ever. Because he is truly free to love himself and life again!

At the very same moment we were overcome with *grief* at the loss of Hunter on this earth, Hunter was overcome with *joy* because he was —and will forever be—in the presence of God and Jesus!

Since July 15, 2017, Romans 4:20-21 (NIV) has become my life verse. "Yet he (she) did not waver through unbelief regarding the **promise** of God, but was strengthened in his (her) faith and gave glory to God, being fully persuaded that God had power to do what he had promised."

God's will be done!

Next Level Faith

◦ *Bruce* ◦

In life there will always be a battle to fight. We are born into it. And there is always an enemy. But there is also One who is greater than the battle and the enemy, and His promise is that He will never leave us nor forsake us. As Sandy and I were fighting the greatest battle of our lives, we were also growing greatly in our faith. Our greatest sanctuary was usually our screened-in porch where we would sit for hours praying and seeking God's guidance. As we positioned ourselves to hear from the Lord, He answered individually and collectively. He gave us great and precious promises. But He also asked something that tested the very core of our faith: "Do you trust Me, and will you accept My will over yours?" With careful deliberation and resolve, Sandy and I both committed to stop praying for what we wanted and began praying, "Not my will, but yours Lord." It did not fix the problem, but it began to give us something more powerful. It delivered us from being consumed by worry, fear, doubt, anxiety, anger and control, and replaced it with God's presence, peace, power and overwhelming love and joy - no matter the circumstances. Now, in the middle of the storms, we could rejoice!

"Rejoice in the Lord always. I will say it again: Rejoice! ... And the peace of God, which transcends all understanding, will guard your hearts and your minds in Christ Jesus."

Philippians 4:4-7 (NIV)

On July 29th, 2016, I attended a two-day prayer vigil at my home church and was given a blank bookmark. Our pastor encouraged us to write on it whatever God shared with us and to continually pray over it, trusting it was from God. Here is exactly what I wrote:

"Let Go. Believe. Fight. Celebrate. Death is coming and so the Resurrection. I am about to move you from bondage to freedom. You will remember this time. Believe. You are Free!!! Go!!! Be the

Blessing!!! Keep vigil to honor God for generations to come. You will see the deliverance of the Lord. Take off the grave clothes and let him go."

At the time, I didn't know exactly what He was saying, but I knew it was from God and that He would reveal more to me according to His will and in His time. As it turned out, it released supernatural power into Sandy's life and mine - another blessing before we even needed it.

A year later, on July 15th, 2017, Sandy and I had just arrived in Huntersville, an hour from Hickory, for a family gathering at our niece's house when we received a call from Hunter's phone. It was a young lady telling us that Hunter was unconscious on the floor of his apartment and she didn't know what to do. I told her to call "911" for an ambulance and that Sandy and I would return to Hickory immediately. In the pouring rain, I sped and we both prayed. While driving, I experienced a strange combination of "fearing the worst" and "overwhelming peace." In the meantime, I called a friend who lived nearby and asked if he could go to the apartment and let me know what was happening.

There was no word.

When we arrived, the police met us in the street outside Hunter's apartment and told us that our son was deceased.

Sandy collapsed in the middle of the road and began sobbing and crying out to God. I held her and prayed.

On July 16th, 2017, the day after our son went on to be with the Lord, Sandy and I were sitting in the sanctuary of our porch. Sandy began to speak to God, "I don't understand this, God. You gave me your promise that Hunter would be OK. This doesn't look OK. I trust you. Help me understand your promise."

I didn't know what to say, so I simply pulled the bookmark God gave me a year earlier and began to pray through the words I had written.

"Let Go. Believe. Fight. Celebrate.
Death is coming and so the Resurrection..."

At that, Sandy immediately began to praise God. As I prayed those words from the bookmark God revealed to her the meaning and significance of His promise. "Hunter's better than OK. He's with Me. He's free and so are you."

We celebrated in God's love and in His truth that Hunter would never struggle again but was now "loving life" like never before - another great gift and blessing from God.

Perspective is Everything

◦ *Ethan* ◦

I don't know what you put your faith in, or where you are in your faith journey, but it's important for you to know that I love Jesus because He first loved me, and I look to Him as my reference point. I realize my view may differ from yours, and that's OK. However, I encourage you to keep an open mind as you read. Although our stories and faith journeys are different, I believe we all have more in common than we think. This is what makes community so beautiful and our stories so powerful.

The reason I will forever seek, follow, and thank Jesus is because I've experienced His unconditional love in my own life. He has been, is currently, and will always be there for me. My own story starts out very similarly to Hunter's. Despite accepting Jesus' love and grace at a young age, I rebelled against Him throughout high school and college. Thinking back, I can't tell you the reason why - other than we are all innately selfish people. My selfishness may manifest itself differently than yours, but one is no worse than the other because it all ultimately hinders us from living out our purpose. We were created for relationships - first with God, and then with others. Selfishness is the biggest hindrance to living that out. To this day my greatest vice is convenience. It's so much easier not to worry about purpose, to chase instant and temporary satisfaction, and to disregard the needs of others.

This was never more evident than in my earlier rebellious years when I escaped responsibility by partying. The more I chose selfishness over love, and ease and convenience over purpose and intentionality, the more I needed to numb my convictions with sex, alcohol, and weed. Hence, my spiral.

Several years of this attitude and lifestyle eventually pushed me to my breaking point on the last day of my first semester as a sophomore at UNCW. After bombing my last final exam, I was coming off a high, just sitting in my car in the school parking lot, when out of nowhere I began to drown in disappointment, anxiety, sorrow, guilt, depression and complete lostness. It was as if all the years of numbness had been built into a tidal wave of emotions and crashed over me at once. I felt alone and broken. I couldn't do anything but sit and sob. And as I did, rain began to pour down in dramatic fashion. I have never felt more isolated in my life than in that moment.

Then, right there in the midst of my darkest moment, I heard a voice from my perfect heavenly Dad asking, "Ethan, where are you?" I had no answer, but it didn't matter. God was there. I was not alone. And right then, hope and grace rushed in and I was overwhelmed with the realization of how much I was loved by my perfect heavenly Dad despite my rebellious, self-centered choices. The awareness of His presence and love broke me even further, but in the best way possible.

God wasn't waiting on me to have my life together. He wasn't disappointed, nor was He trying to fix me. He was just there and fully present. In that moment, the God of the universe intimately cared for and comforted me. I will never forget it.

I'd like to say from that day on my life was easy and painless. However, just because God met me that day and I rededicated my life to Him while on the phone with my dad, the transformation was not a cakewalk. Life is simple, but it is not easy. My struggles didn't just disappear. My relationships weren't restored overnight, and my choices didn't immediately change. What did change that day —and has continued to grow over time— was my relationship with God and my perspective moving forward. And these two things are what got me through the most tragic experience of my life: losing my little brother and best friend.

Like all brothers, we fought and annoyed each other, but Hunter and I were best friends. Ever since Mom and Dad first introduced "pizza n' movie night" back when we were young, one of our favorite things to do together was watch movies. We would have our own movie marathons: spending hours binge-watching movies and shows (even before Netflix made binging cool). The other thing Hunter and I loved was humor. We loved laughing and making everyone around us laugh. We also had the same type of humor and always fed off one another the way only two brothers could. Our love for movies and contagious humor made for some very entertaining movie-quoting sessions which turned into "not-sure-what-we're-even-laughing-at" sessions.

These are just a couple of things that bonded Hunter and me and created some of my favorite memories. Memories that stir up joy, happiness, and laughter.

But then there are the *other* memories. Memories that stir up anger, sadness, bitterness and hurt. Memories of Dad and I looking all over a hotel and beach for Hunter on what was supposed to be a fun weekend getaway for our friends' wedding, only to find him completely out of his mind, barely functioning, and talking nonsense in the hallway. Memories of the ramifications Hunter's poor choices had as this disease continued to take over. Memories of Mom in her closet, face down, on her knees sobbing after Hunter had stormed out of the house. Hurt, broken and afraid, she continued to beg

God to help him despite the fact that he'd seemingly chosen drugs over us - again. Memories of Hunter not being in my wedding because, just days before, he chose to skip our family vacation to stay in Hickory and use drugs. These are the memories that hurt most because I had to watch Hunter throw his life away while also seeing my parents in agonizing pain over their baby boy. What fed my bitterness the most was the thought of Hunter refusing to see the pain, burden and sorrow his choices were causing.

In the midst of these painful memories there were glimpses of hope, but with it came doubt and second-guessing. I wanted to be there for him and help him make right choices. I so desperately wanted Hunter to have the same experience and story of reconciliation God had given me, but the more my attempts to help failed, the more bitter I became.

So what was I supposed to do? How could I relieve some of my parents' burden? How do I not hate this brother I loved so much? How do I deal with him not being in my life anymore? How do I heal from years of hurt? How do I refuse to take the wide road of a convenient, selfish and bitter attitude?

Just as God was faithful to meet me in my own dark moment years ago, he has also helped me work through two main questions that have challenged and changed my perspective.

First, how am I supposed to have enough love for someone after being hurt by them so often? *How did Jesus?* The answer: stay connected to the source of love. As a flawed, imperfect, selfish human being, I will never have the capacity in my own strength to love unconditionally. Jesus was fully human, so He felt all the emotions and pain we feel; but He remained connected to the Father, the only true source of unconditional love. I had been offered that same connection with God, my source of unconditional love. I just had to realize it was available, then experience, embrace, and protect it. His unconditional love is what forever changed my life that rainy day in Wilmington and every day since. It's what fills me up when I'm struggling with selfishness and fear and continues to spare me from a miserable, self-centered life.

I've learned that loving someone unconditionally can be hard and painful. It requires us to meet someone where they're at - not wait until they have everything together or get where we want them to be. It is loving someone whether or not they love us in return.

Nothing of unconditional love is without pain or discomfort. There was no way I could love Hunter like this without being connected to the source of unconditional love and experiencing it for myself first. There is so much pain, suffering, and heartache in this life that doesn't just go away and shouldn't be ignored. It has to be dealt with. The challenge is to do so without allowing bitterness to seep in.

This leads me to my second question: how do I avoid becoming bitter toward someone I love who has repeatedly chosen ease, convenience and vices over love, being together, and relationship? *How did Jesus?* The answer is found in understanding choices. First, we make our own choices, but we do not control the choices of others. Second, while I cannot choose my emotions, I can choose my reactions to them. My perspective is a choice. Bitterness is a choice. Love is a choice. Jesus experienced emotions just like us but intentionally chose to love the people society deemed "unlovable." And He also loved the people that hurt Him. How did He avoid becoming bitter? He disassociated their choices from His unwavering love for them. Jesus realized that choices are not people. I can hate someone's choices and still love the person.

But here's the thing about choices. They all have consequences, either good or bad. Whether at my worst or best, my choices had consequences that affected my relationship with God, my family and my unconditional love for my brother. The same applied to Hunter. At his worst or best, there were consequences for himself, his family, and even his life.

Regardless of the consequences, our love for Hunter never changed, and neither did Jesus' love for him ... or me. Since Jesus' love is not tied to outcomes and is unconditional, the same should be said of me. God has been there for me at my darkest moments, so why shouldn't I do the same for others?

Throughout these experiences I learned something that will forever change the way I live my life: the importance of *gratitude*. Choosing a heart of gratitude has altered my perspective and inspires me to love and live with more freedom, fewer expectations and a greater understanding of God's radical love.

Gratitude is one of the most powerful and sustainable forms of motivation. If I'm grateful for Hunter (in both good and bad times) then I can face the hurt and pain and overcome it, because ultimately, it draws me closer to God. I am grateful for the loss because love and joy have outweighed it. I am grateful because I know where Hunter is and that he will never have to struggle again. I am grateful for the growth in my relationships with God, my wife, and my parents. I am grateful for the opportunity to experience peace amidst a tragedy. I am grateful for the privilege of witnessing Mom and Dad live out their faith in a way that will impact me and my future family forever. I am grateful for a God who loves me so individually and genuinely... Who wants to be with me in my darkest times, my best times, and the little moments in between. I am grateful for vulnerability and for experiencing the pain because now I cherish love, joy and peace even more. I am grateful for a perfect heavenly Father whose love doesn't change because of what I do or don't do. All He wants is to be with me.

This truth seems so simple, but simple and easy are not the same thing. I've definitely learned this the hard way, and I'm grateful for it, because anything of value is worth the fight. Gratitude is the essence of worship, and that's how I want to live my life.

Gratitude gives me the ability to experience grief the way God intended. One of my mentors compared grief to the Grand Canyon. It's magnificent, powerful, mysterious, awe-inspiring. You want to get as close to the edge as possible to drink in all of its beauty and power, but you also don't want to fall in. Choosing gratitude in all things allows me the opportunity to experience grief the way God intended, without falling into a pit of despair or hopelessness.

Through the grief, pain, selfishness and rebellion, I've learned this: throughout our finite, earthly life, we need to embrace all our emotions because they bring knowledge of God's grace, mercy, forgiveness and love.

And His love is worth it!

Seeing the Why

◇ *Sandy* ◇

I f we are being completely honest with ourselves, there is one question we all ask God... WHY?

- Why is this happening?
- Why did God allow it to happen?
- Why did it have to happen this way?
- Why, God?

We will never comprehend all the "why's" this side of heaven, but we can take comfort in knowing God does.

The Promise

"Great is our Lord and mighty in power;
his understanding has no limit."

Psalms 147:5 (NIV)

Our family does not understand all the reasons why God chose to take Hunter, but as I noted before, one clear reason is God's deep love for him. He gave Hunter freedom from his bondage and is teaching our family how to live in that freedom as well.

As I share some of the following stories, I hope you can appreciate a few more of the "why's" God has revealed through Hunter's life and death.

As we were planning Hunter's celebration of life service, God told me He wanted me to share my hummingbird story. Bruce, Ethan and Jesse also felt compelled to speak. We knew it was going to be one of the hardest and most difficult things any of us has ever had to do, but we were going to be obedient and trust God with the outcome. At the church, as I started walking toward the building, my whole body began to shake. I felt like I was going to pass out. I thought, "I can hardly walk. How on earth am I going to get up in front of everyone and speak?" But as we were escorted to our seats, I heard the most precious sound... It was Hunter's voice. You see, the day before, I had requested to have one of the songs Hunter had written and recorded to play while the family

44

was being seated. At the time, I wasn't sure why I felt such an urgency to do that, but now it makes perfect sense. Because the moment I heard Hunter singing and saw his picture displayed on stage, all my anxiety, fear and trembling disappeared, and I was able to stand in front of everyone and share God's love through my hummingbird promise.

Hunter's Song Played at the Celebration

Sandy's Celebration Testimony

There were nearly a thousand family and friends who attended the celebration. Our family felt very blessed by all the love and support. It was definitely God ordained through the beautiful worship music, Hunter's songs and the stories that were shared. That evening at least fourteen people accepted Christ and many others ask for prayer. It's amazing how God took something so painful and agonizing and turned it into a beautiful testimony of His love, joy, peace and hope.

The Promise

A mom of one of Hunter's close friends from high school drove seven hours to come to the celebration. I had not talked to her in six years since they moved out of state when the boys were juniors. A few weeks after the celebration, she sent this letter:

Bruce & Sandy,

I wanted to start by saying that I am so very sorry, and I wish I could take all your pain and grief away. You and your family are in my thoughts and prayers.

I feel compelled to write this letter to let you know how much I respect and look up to the strength you both have. I admire faith and belief in life and God. I have been very weak and angry with life and sometimes God that my life has not exactly gone the way I wanted or that it was the way I wanted for my kids.

I know I am in control of my life but sometimes it seemed easier to be upset with God for not hearing my prayers. I thought to myself if God was so good how could he take my beautiful boys and let their lives get so off track. How could He let my oldest son be so reckless and have an alcohol addiction and be so mad at me daily. I thought constantly, "what have I done wrong to deserve this"! I know you know the struggle and I'm sorry that you had to endure it too. He was able to break part of the vicious cycle with weed and other drugs and I was hoping the alcohol would come along with that, but the addiction and recklessness is still there. It affects all areas of his life and our relationship. Our relationship can be very volatile at moments. I have wanted to give up on him many times, I feel ashamed to admit that. It's exhausting as you know.

I am writing to tell you that I left Hunter's celebration of life not angry at God anymore. His mission and your strength have allowed me to let go of my anger and accept God back into my life. It's not God's fault my beautiful son has his issues and it's not God's fault my life may not have gone the way I planned. I realize I need to have faith in His plan for all of us. I realize I need to not accept Him out of convenience or to only pray when I think I need Him most. I need to accept Him fully and in every aspect of my life.

I'm writing to thank you for giving me the strength to be a better person and understanding of how I need to change my life for the better. I heard the message and mission of change. I have already thanked Hunter. I told him he is reaching people!!!

Thank you both for being exactly who you are...

Several people have told me that Hunter had an integral part of them—or someone they knew—coming to know Jesus. So even with all of Hunter's ups and downs, dark valleys and struggles, God is using his story to impact lives for eternity.

As much as I miss my baby boy, I know God is using Hunter's passing and our brokenness for His glory and that brings me unexplainable joy and peace through it all.

I may not understand all the "why's", but I trust in God's sovereignty.

"... As I have planned, so it will be,
as I have purposed, so it will happen."

Isaiah 14:24 (NIV)

The Other Side
of the Bookmark

◇ *Bruce* ◇

On July 30th, 2016, on the other side of the bookmark, God had me write, "Did I not tell you that if you believe, you will see the glory of God?" John 11:40 (NIV). God has continued to whisper these words into my ear and even more, I have and continue to see His glory.

Three months after Hunter went on to be with the Lord, I was driving to the gym around 5:00 AM for an early Friday morning workout. My mind was not on Hunter. Since I was going to be on the elliptical machine for a twenty-minute warmup, I asked God what I should be praying about during that time. His response was so quick and clear it took me by surprise.

"Ask Me about your son."

I immediately started crying, overwhelmed that God simply wanted to talk to me about my son who was now with Him. My time on the elliptical machine was one of the greatest times of worship and praise I had ever known. God met me there, held me and talked to me about "our" son. He spoke to me about how He'd created Hunter with the spirit of a warrior (and was he ever), but now he's fighting alongside God on my behalf. While God was speaking, I was listening to music. Every song had a warrior theme. What love from this radical God who speaks so intimately - another great gift and blessing from God.

The following Sunday in church we were finishing up a series on spiritual warfare. The message was extremely powerful. As we were worshiping in song and praise toward the end of the service, I could feel the strong presence of God. When I opened my eyes and looked up, I saw Hunter looking down at us. He didn't possess his earthly physical body. I would describe it as translucent. There was no denying it was Hunter. He had the spirit of a warrior - strong, powerful, angelic and transcendent.

As you can imagine, I was overwhelmed by Hunter's presence and in awe of God's love. Quite honestly, I wasn't sure if or how I was going to share this with Sandy. Back in the car after the service, Sandy turned to me and said she couldn't really explain it, but she felt Hunter's presence with us during the worship service. I told her about seeing Hunter. We cried and praised God. It was another great gift and blessing.

The following weekend we traveled with some close friends back to Roan Mountain to enjoy fellowship, recreation and respite. What we'd always considered a place to retreat had now become a great sanctuary the Lord had given us. The last time we'd visited, it had been about a week after Hunter's passing when our family traveled there to spread his ashes. By the Divine leading of Almighty God and in His presence, we'd released them into the rushing stream over the fourth of five bridges on the property. It was quite the experience - hard but beautiful!

The Saturday morning of this particular weekend with our friends, God continued to radically demonstrate His love and His fulfillment of promises. I got up before daybreak and hiked to the fourth bridge (Hunter's bridge). As I approached it, the sun was just rising up over the mountain and shining in the exact place where we had spread Hunter's ashes. The water was strong, deep and dark, the current split by a large boulder sitting immediately next to the bridge. As I gazed on the spot where the sun was shining, I caught a glimpse of something glistening in the water. Cautiously, I climbed down onto the boulder, reached into the water and pulled out a knife. A warrior knife! Hidden in the dark rushing water where it could not be seen without the help of the sun's illuminating light.

Overwhelmed by God's love and His goodness once again, I wept. Understandably, Sandy and our friends were astonished, and together, we celebrated another of God's great gifts and blessings.

Gifts of Love

◦ *Sandy* ◦

"For God so loved the world that he gave his one and only Son, that whoever believes in him shall not perish but have eternal life."

John 3:16 (NIV)

God has given the ultimate love gift of eternal life through His Son, Jesus Christ, for those who choose to accept Him. If you have never made that decision and allowed Him to be Lord of your life, then I encourage you to respond to His invitation today. Heaven and hell are real places and the choice you make now will affect where you spend eternity - either together with God or forever apart from Him.

If you have accepted Jesus, then God wants to bless you with many other gifts and blessings, but you have to put yourself in position to receive them however God chooses.

Since Hunter's passing, God has showered me with many precious gifts. At times, it has been overwhelming but in a good way. As you read about several of these love gifts, I hope you will see God's radical love and be inspired to look for His blessings in your own story.

After sharing my hummingbird story at Hunter's celebration of life service, so many people sent me texts and/or photos of their own first-time hummingbird encounters. They were so touched and moved by God's presence and realness through His promise.

Bruce and I received a letter entitled "Blades for Wings" written by one of Hunter's longtime childhood friends. In it, he shared his own hummingbird story from the summer before Hunter passed. He was working at a fine dining restaurant in the mountains of North Carolina. The restaurant had direct exposure to the outside. Hummingbirds would fly in and get stuck in the high ceiling, exhausting themselves while trying to escape. On several occasions the tiny creatures would collapse and fall to the floor. He would take them in hand, make a sugar solution and nurse them back to health. That summer he became known as the "Hummingbird Whisperer." He was completely unaware of the relationship between hummingbirds and Hunter until he attended the celebration of life and heard my hummingbird promise.

I have had multiple hummingbirds trapped in our garage at the same window where the first appeared. I have held all of them until they rested enough to take flight again.

In the garage one morning, I encountered a hummingbird. That same evening, I watched a movie that featured a main character whose last name was Hunter. In the film, he gave the woman he loved a hummingbird ornament.

The Promise

In honor of Hunter's twenty-fourth birthday (five months after his passing), I wanted to give him a love gift that would make him smile and bring laughter to his heart. It needed to be something radical and out of the ordinary in order to show my love for him. So... I decided to get a tattoo! Maybe for you that might not be a big deal, but for me it was definitely out of my comfort zone. I used to threaten Ethan and Hunter that if they ever got a tattoo, the wrath of Mama Bear would be upon them. While it was a running joke with us, I really meant it. Being perfectly honest, I despised tattoos and was judgmental toward people who had them. But God has a way of humbling us to see the truth, because the truth will set us free. And today I have a beautiful ruby-throated hummingbird tattooed on my right wrist (Oh, the irony!). Underneath it reads, "God's Promise." I'd love to hear Hunter's response to my decision, but that will have to wait until I see him again.

I was driving down the road one day listening to a song on one of the Christian radio stations. It had a great upbeat sound and the lyrics made me think of Hunter. I imagined him dancing and singing in heaven alongside Jesus. As I came to a stop light I continued to sing and raise my hands, thanking God that Hunter was with Him. I glanced over at a large white utility truck that had pulled up beside me at the intersection and couldn't believe my eyes. There on the side of the truck in big bold letters was the name, "HUNTER." In response, I cried out for joy at God's faithfulness and His promises.

Bruce and I befriended a gentleman from Puerto Rico since Hunter's passing. He had never met Hunter but had seen pictures and knew our story. He said Hunter came to him in a dream (speaking English) twice in the same night and asked him to relay a message to us. Hunter said, "Please tell my parents to stop crying over me, that I am good, and am where I'm supposed to be." After the dream, our friend woke up immediately and just sat and cried for several hours because he felt God's presence and spirit so strong in Hunter. As he finished sharing details of the dream, Bruce asked him what time this took place. He said 3:00 AM Friday morning. Bruce shared with him that he, too, was awoken at 3:00 AM and couldn't go back to sleep. From this experience, I realized God can speak and move in ways that are sometimes hard to comprehend and even harder for us to believe. He chooses how and when He wants to communicate and it's up to us to choose to receive it or not.

On Jan 30, 2019, I traveled alone to Roan Mountain, Tennessee to begin the process of writing this book. When I made the reservation the only cabin available was the same one our family stayed in over Father's Day with Hunter in 2017 with all the hummingbird décor. We had not stayed in that cabin since that time. As I approached the cabin door, I dreaded all the memories and emotions that would come flooding back. But when I entered, I couldn't believe my eyes. It was immediately evident that God had gone before me... as He always does! When I opened the door my hesitant gaze fell on a beautiful, remodeled cabin where everything had been made new! God is so good! He'd given Hunter a *new* life and me a *new* cabin to begin my writing journey. A few days earlier my Bible study devotion was entitled *New Life.* The scripture reference was 2 Corinthians 5:17 (NKJV) which reads, "Therefore, if anyone is in Christ, he is a new creation; old things have passed away; behold, all things have become new." That day God confirmed Hunter has a new life. The reassurance brought me such comfort and peace.

The bedroom wall where a hummingbird picture once hung, now holds a new picture with one of my life verses written on it: "Be still and know..." Psalms 46:10 (NIV).

This cabin has become my favorite because it reminds me of His promise: God has made all things new!

Remember the warrior knife Bruce found in the water exactly where we spread Hunter's ashes? Well, now I've got my own. On my birthday in 2019, I told Bruce I wanted to go and spend  the day hanging out in Black Mountain and Asheville, two of our favorite mountain towns to visit. While walking around downtown Asheville, it began to rain so we sought shelter in the Mast General Store and waited it out. As Bruce went to look at rain gear, I walked over to a glass display counter that held all shapes and sizes of knives. I am not one to migrate toward knives but, for some reason, interest stirred inside me that day. Among the various selections, one particular knife caught my eye. It looked like a smaller replica of the warrior knife that Bruce had found in the water. Leaning to get a better look, I noticed writing on the blade. The inscription on it caused my heart to skip a beat. It read, "UP and AT 'EM", a phrase very similar to the title of the last song Hunter recorded before he passed entitled "Up and Adam" - Different spelling, but God has a sense of humor. Needless to say, I got a knife that day for my birthday. Thank you, God and Hunter, for my special gift!

Up and Adam Song

This poem is a beautiful gift one of my dear friends wrote in honor of Hunter.

God saw the constant battle
That you tried to fight
He knew deep down inside your heart
You desired what was right.
Your desire was to be an example
To those with demons all around
You shared your music freely

Joy Through the Brokenness

In hopes Christ would be found.
To those who looked on from outside
You were always full of smiles
Even when deep in your heart
You battled ferocious trials.
With every trial and battle scar
You were determined to win the fight
You'd fall down, then get back up
And seek to find the light.
Your heart's desire was to live just and pure
And to find your way
And now just as God promised the battle's over
You're released & you're OK.

Why Couldn't I
Save My Son?

◇ *Bruce* ◇

In Matthew 27:45-46 (NIV), Jesus said, "Eli, Eli, lema sabachthani?" which means, "My God, my God, why have you forsaken me?"

The darkest day of my life was when the police officer told us that our son was deceased. The darkest days in my soul were when I questioned, "Why could I not save my son?" These were the days when I wondered if God had forsaken or withheld something from me. Perhaps I didn't do something I was supposed to do. God had proven His love to me and my family over and over again, but why would He not save my son? This question cut to the core of my identity and my beliefs. But God didn't leave me in despair.

God loved us enough to give His Son (John 3:16). Jesus loved His father enough to lay down His own life for us (Romans 5:8). God also asks if we love Him enough to lay down our lives for His purpose, His kingdom, His glory and His people. But do we love God this much? Do *I* love God this much? Would I lay down my own life for Him? Even more so, would I give my own son for others if this is God's will?

God never did forsake His Son that day on the cross. But He did let Him die so that my son Hunter might be saved. "He who did not spare his own Son, but gave Him up for us all – how will he not also, along with him, graciously give us all things?" Romans 8:32 (NIV)

Through this scripture promise God eventually and definitively answered my question. It was not my place to save my son. It was His. It was my place to bring him to Jesus so that he might receive that which had been promised. And with that I was faithful. My son knew Jesus as his personal Savior and now he knows the freedom and peace of that salvation. Hunter may not have won the battle on earth, but death doesn't have the last say on his life. His heavenly Father decided otherwise. This is the hope that rises daily in my soul and replaces the despair with a song of praise and gratitude.

Through it All

◦ *Sandy* ◦

A few days after Hunter's passing, one of my friends gave me an inspirational book as a gift. As I read, God impressed upon me the word *"through"*, a perfect characterization of His all-consuming love. Throughout the Bible it is used to display His power, His love and His grace.

No matter what we are struggling with... loss of a loved one, addiction, depression, marital, financial, or health issues... God can and will get us through it, but we have to do our part to *let go* and take that *step of faith* to trust God with the outcome of our story.

Through the Red Sea

"Then Moses stretched out his hand over the sea, and all that night the LORD drove the sea back with a strong east wind and turned it into dry land. The waters were divided, and the Israelites went through the sea on dry ground, with a wall of water on their right and on their left."

Exodus 14:21-22 (NIV)

Please take a moment to visualize what is happening in this scene. God is making a way for His people, but they had to take a step of faith (into the sea) and trust God to get them through it. God didn't instruct the Israelites to go over or around the sea. His instructions were for them to go through it in order to receive the blessings awaiting them on the other side.

What blessings may be awaiting you on the other side? Are you <u>willing</u> to take that step of faith and find out?

Through the Waters and Fire

"When you pass through the waters,
I will be with you; and through the rivers,
they shall not overwhelm you;
when you walk through fire
you shall not be burned,
and the flame shall not consume you."

Isaiah 43:2 (ESV)

This verse should bring us comfort knowing God is with us when we pass through the rivers of difficulty and the fires of oppression. And that means we're going to be OK.

Does your life reflect this type of
Peace that surpasses all understanding?

Through the Valley of the Shadow of Death

"Even though I walk through the darkest valley,
I will fear no evil, for you are with me;
your rod and your staff, they comfort me."

Psalms 23:4 (NIV)

No matter what this crazy world or Satan, the father of lies, tries to do to God's children, God will provide a way through our darkest valleys.

Hunter's passing has provided an opportunity for our family to share our faith and bless others through the darkest moments of our lives. What Satan meant for evil in the loss of our son here on earth, God has turned into a beautiful love story.

My hope and prayer is that you have experienced God's all-consuming love as you have walked with our family in the journey to find *Joy Through the Brokenness.*

God's love is real and personal. He loves you and has a plan and a purpose for your life. If you believe this, I want to leave you with a thought-provoking —and critical—question...

Are you willing to trust God and
allow Him to write your <u>own</u> story?

GOD'S WILL BE DONE!

*"Destiny: It's the unrevealed
reason for life and reason for death."*

Hunter Schronce

Made in the USA
Columbia, SC
24 August 2020